Original title:
Cedar Sap and Sonnets

Copyright © 2025 Creative Arts Management OÜ
All rights reserved.

Author: Liam Sterling
ISBN HARDBACK: 978-1-80567-274-6
ISBN PAPERBACK: 978-1-80567-573-0

Nature's Tale, Rich in Sap

In the woods where the night critters play,
A sticky surprise leads the squirrels astray.
They prance with delight, with goo on their paws,
What a sticky situation, oh, the laughter that guffaws!

The owls are all hooting, quite puzzled for sure,
As they watch the whole scene, it's hard to endure.
One owl drops a twig, oh what a big flop,
The critters all giggle, will this madness ever stop?

A raccoon joins in with a cap on his head,
He slips in the goo, almost falls on his spread.
He grumbles and grunts, as he wipes on a tree,
"Next time I'll bring snacks, that's the key to be free!"

The woodpecker chuckles, with beak on a bark,
"What's all this ruckus? You're making a mark!"
With laughter all around, they embrace the good fun,
In the land rich with gunk, where mischief has won!

Echoes of the Timbered Verse

In the forest, trees do chatter,
Their gossip brings a lot of laughter.
A squirrel's tale, a bird's remark,
Leaves rustle as they make their spark.

Woodpeckers drum like a band gone wild,
While pine cones plop, oh, nature's child.
The rhythm here is quite absurd,
As branches dance, not saying a word.

The Scent of Spruce and Stanzas

Amidst the boughs, the air so sweet,
The forest's charm can't be beat.
A wiggly worm recites a rhyme,
While crickets chirp in perfect time.

Twigs take turns on a tiny stage,
Performing lines of woodland rage.
Even the ants march in a line,
Sing about their grand design.

Melodies in the Shade of Cones

In shady nooks, we find a tune,
With melodies that make us swoon.
A mouse with dreams and big ambitions,
Composes songs with sly conditions.

The owls hoot with a wise old jest,
While fungi get invited as guests.
Mushrooms sway to the woodland beat,
As vines and branches share a seat.

Tales Woven in Pine Needles

With needles soft, the tales unfold,
Of critters brave and hearts so bold.
The raccoon's prank, the fox's wink,
The world of trees is full of ink.

A hedgehog's laugh, a beetle's dance,
Couples twirl in a leafy trance.
Each story told beneath the stars,
Echoes deep, they're never far.

Poetic Embers in the Glade

In the forest, roots tango,
Squirrels wear tiny hats,
Trees chuckle to the breeze,
While the owl spills some chats.

Bunnies hop with flair,
Throwing leaves in the air,
Moss cushions the silly dance,
Each step a silly chance.

The brook giggles awake,
With fish wearing capes,
Sunlight bursts into laughter,
As shadows play their pranks.

Under the twinkling stars,
Nature hosts a ball,
Crickets croon the tunes,
Oh, what a wild call!

In the Arms of the Evergreen

Hug a tree, just because,
They won't mind the squeeze,
Branches sway in delight,
Dancing rather at ease.

Breezes whisper sweet jokes,
While ferns shake with glee,
Even the rocks chip in,
Cracking smiles, can't you see?

Birds in a choir sing loud,
Their notes like silly tweets,
Each puddle reflects joy,
As the fun beats repeat.

In this grove of delight,
Laughter floats held high,
Join the symphony here,
Beneath the brightening sky!

Lyrical Echoes of the Forest

The woods spill tales of jest,
With mushrooms in full bloom,
Deer prance like they're on stage,
In this quirky little room.

Glowing fireflies respond,
With their dance so neat,
Light up the curious paths,
Where every critter meets.

Barking trees share secrets,
As squirrels craft their schemes,
They dream and giggle bright,
In their forest of dreams.

A splash of folly here,
With leaves that pop and twirl,
Join this frolicsome ball,
In nature, let's all whirl!

Ode to the Whispering Woods

A breeze of giggles wafts,
Through branches high and low,
The trunks all crack a smile,
With every little blow.

Streamers of tendril vines,
Join in on the fun spree,
While the bushes gossip loud,
About the wise old tree.

Squirrels wearing big clown shoes,
Join the woodland fringe,
Raccoons with funky hats,
In a mischievous hinge.

Under a canopy bright,
Where shadows dance in cool,
Nature's laughter echoes wide,
In this whimsical school!

The Woodsman's Ballad of Nature

In the woods where laughter reigns,
The trees dance like they've got no chains.
A squirrel puts on a tiny show,
While chipmunks hum a tune, you know.

The old owl hoots a funny joke,
As branches sway, the leaves provoke.
The forest floor is a lively stage,
Where every creature acts their age.

A beaver's grin is wide and bold,
While the rabbits gossip tales of old.
Nature's party is such a blast,
Even the mushrooms are having a laugh!

So grab your hat, let's take a stroll,
In this wild place where joy takes hold.
With nature's choir and fun galore,
We'll dance through life, forevermore.

Saplings Swaying in Harmony

Little trees in a grassy line,
Playing tricks in the sunshine.
With roots that wiggle and leaves that clap,
They hold a dance that's a joyful trap.

The ants parade with tiny feet,
While young branches sway to the beat.
The sunbeams giggle as they peek,
And tickle the saplings, oh so sleek.

In circles they twist, roots all askew,
Inviting butterflies, they'd fly through.
Every twig tells a joke or two,
While mossy mats take a comfy cue.

So here we gather, a fun brigade,
In a leafy land where we all played.
With giggles echoing all around,
In this merry grove where joy is found.

The Lure of Timeless Timber Tales

Gather 'round, let's spin a yarn,
Of lumberjacks and trees with charm.
With axes swinging, they tell their tales,
Of tangles, fumbles, and big old fails.

A tree once whispered, "Take it slow!"
While the woodman danced and stubbed his toe.
With every log, a funny story,
Of nature's secrets and all its glory.

So why not sit on a sturdy stump,
And laugh out loud, give your heart a thump.
For nature's bounty is full of cheer,
With every trunk, a tale to leer.

The forest echoes with quirky glee,
As we recount our history.
In woods where spirits frolic free,
Nature's laughter sings to you and me.

Lyrical Breezes Through Pine Boughs

The wind whispers softly, jokes in air,
With pine needles rustling, a comedic flair.
A gust rolls in with a playful sigh,
It tickles the trees, oh my, oh my!

Branches sway with a wink and nod,
While the groundhog chuckles, clapping his paw.
Squirrels ride in on a breezy wave,
Chasing one another, oh so brave.

The sun peeks down, it's a warm delight,
Casting shadows that dance in the light.
Every twig is a punchline keen,
In this woodland stage, a lively scene.

So join the frolic, don't be shy,
Let nature's giggles lift you high.
With laughter swirling in every leaf,
Here's where we find our hearts in relief.

Under the Canopy's Spell

In a forest where the squirrels play,
Leaves dance in a comical sway.
A raccoon wears a hat so grand,
Sipping tea with a tiny band.

Bugs wiggle like they've lost their tune,
Spiders knit underneath the moon.
The owls hoot in a funny tone,
In this leafy world, they've made it home.

The Breathing Grove

Trees whisper secrets to the breeze,
Chatting gently, like old peas.
A woodpecker is quite the artist,
Knocking beats, he's truly the hardest.

Frogs croak jokes that make birds cackle,
While chipmunks race – a speedy battle.
Every creature shows their flair,
In this breathing grove, there's laughter to share.

A Symphony of Roots and Branches

Beneath the ground, roots start to dance,
Putting on quite the wild romance.
Branches scribble silly rhymes,
Tickling trunks with laughter chimes.

A family of owls throws a bash,
While hedgehogs roll in a tipsy crash.
The wind plays tunes that make them sing,
In this symphony, joy is everything.

Tales from the Timbered Realm

In the timbered realm where trouble brews,
Rabbits wear boots and sing the blues.
Trees tell tales with creaky laughs,
While bees take breaks for photos and graphs.

A fox claims he's the forest's king,
But really just loves to dance and swing.
Laughter echoes through the dark,
As critters plot their next silly spark.

Nature's Lyrical Essence

In woods where whispers dance and sway,
A squirrel jokes in a feathery ballet.
The trees roll their eyes, in leafy delight,
As mushrooms wear hats, a curious sight.

An owl hoots a pun, sharp as a knife,
While rabbits discuss the meaning of life.
With each sprout of green, the giggles arise,
Nature's own stand-up, in disguise.

Stanzas from the Sylvan Depths

Where bees sing in buzzing, rhythmic play,
The flowers have gossip, in bright array.
A frog on a lily, with leaps so spry,
Claims he's the prince, though we know he's shy.

The brook laughs aloud, as rocks join in too,
Spitting out tales, of a fish and a shoe.
While butterflies flit with a dramatic flair,
Each petal's a page, filled with laughter to share.

Ink of Nature

With a quill made of twigs and a blob of gray feast,
The poet inked stories of a snail and a beast.
The grass chuckles softly, swaying its ears,
While ants tell tall tales, filled with giggles and cheers.

The ink spills a verse, about a worm in a boat,
Who sailed through the puddles, on a leaf that could float.
The clouds clap with joy, in a sky painted blue,
As nature scribbles verses, each day something new.

Written in Green

On parchment of leaves, the verses unfold,
A chameleon sings, while the sunset turns gold.
With laughter akin to a tickling breeze,
Even the rocks can't help but tease.

The fern plays its flute, in soft tones of cheer,
As daisies debate, what's the best joke of the year.
Meanwhile, a deer joins the merry affair,
With antlers like crowns, it's quite the grand bear.

Harmony Among the Branches

The rustling leaves share secrets and dreams,
As critters compose their own silly schemes.
A raccoon steals snacks, a bandit at heart,
While the flowers participate, each playing their part.

The whispers are loud in this green-streaked choir,
While butterflies flutter, igniting the fire.
Every branch is a stage, for mischief and fun,
In harmony they laugh, until the day's done.

The Aroma of Verdant Dreams

In a grove where squirrels prance,
The trees hold secrets, a dance.
With scents that tickle your nose,
You wonder what mischief grows.

A raccoon in a top hat, quite dapper,
Jumps around, causing quite the clapper.
The leaves giggle, join the spree,
As nature's jesters run wild and free.

The flowers blush in hues so bright,
Planning a party under the moonlight.
Bees wear shades while buzzin' along,
Every hum a comical song.

Beneath this green and lively theme,
You lose yourself in a dream.
Whimsy wafts from every bend,
Where laughter and nature blend.

Embracing Autumn's Breath

Crunching leaves beneath our shoes,
Autumn whispers funny news.
A squirrel wearing knitted gear,
Says winter's coming, never fear!

Pumpkins laugh with goofy grins,
Waving at fall's merry spins.
Even the acorns crack a joke,
As the woodpecker starts to poke.

The breeze carries a ticklish cheer,
Ruffling hats and sending them here.
A dance of twirls on this clear day,
Nature's humor always at play.

With colors bright and crisp delight,
Every sight is a funny sight.
As trees in scarlet start to sway,
We join their laughter on this day.

Rhythms of the Forest Heart

The forest pulses with a beat,
Where oddball critters meet and greet.
A turtle's slow and steady crawl,
While rabbits race and giggle, enthralled.

Each branch a stage for the birdies to sing,
Swinging their tails like a Broadway fling.
A woodchuck juggles nuts with flair,
As chipmunks cheer without a care.

The owls wear glasses, wise and keen,
Sharing secrets of the unseen.
With a hoot and a chuckle, they play their part,
In the symphony of the forest heart.

Even the daisies start to sway,
In rhythm with the playful fray.
Nature's charm, with a wink and a glance,
Invites us all to join the dance.

Moonlit Canopy Serenade

Under a sky, stars like pebbles,
A raccoon conducts with playful levels.
The moon grins wide, sharing its light,
As shadows flicker, bringing delight.

Crickets chirp a goofy tune,
In harmony with the howling moon.
A firefly flits in a dapper suit,
Winking at flowers, all in pursuit.

Owl and fox hold a duet sublime,
Trading tales of the silliest time.
While shadows dance in a cha-cha swirl,
The night plays on, a magical whirl.

With laughter echoing through the glade,
Every whisper's a mischief parade.
As the forest revels in the night's serenade,
Joy and whimsy shall never fade.

The Lament of the Sylvan Spirit

In a forest where the trees like to sing,
A spirit cried out, 'I forgot my wing!'
The squirrels chuckled and danced all around,
While the owl just hooted, 'That's silly, profound!'

With a branch for a hat, and moss as a tie,
The spirit looked dapper, but started to cry.
"Oh what a bore, with no flight to be found!"
The pinecones rolled over, proclaiming, "Get down!"

As the rains came a-falling and worms played the flutes,
The spirit then wobbled while wearing his boots.
"I'm the fashion of nature, the tree-man so grand!"
But the beetles just laughed, forming an insect band.

In the end, with a stomp and a loud jolly cheer,
The spirit learned laughter is the key to good cheer.
So he gathered the forest, made jokes 'til the night,
And they all ended up in a whimsical flight!

Forest Tales Captured in Verse

Once in a grove where the critters conspire,
A tale was spun like a thick golden wire.
A badger had stolen a rabbit's fine hat,
Then strutted around like a serious brat.

The rabbits convened with winks and loud giggles,
"Let's stage a heist!" one of them wiggles.
With carrots for weapons, they plotted their scheme,
In their warren, they laughed, living out their dream.

Under the moonlight, they marched with great flair,
While the badger just sighed, without a single care.
The heist turned to chaos, a duel ensued,
With hats flying high, and both sides were skewed.

In the end, they all piled in laughter so merry,
The badger apologized, and they shared a berry.
From that day on, the lost hat was adored,
As their forest tales grew, nobody was bored!

Rhapsody of the Sapling Whisper

A sapling once dreamed of being a tree,
"I'm small but mighty! Just wait and see!"
The winds, they just whispered, with giggles and glee,
"Keep dreaming, wee one, in the shade we agree."

As squirrels nearby rolled in the soft grass,
The sapling declared, "I'll grow up so fast!"
But roots got all tangled, and bugs liked to munch,
With each little wiggle, it felt like a punch.

One day a tall oak, grand as he swayed,
Said, "Little friend, don't be so dismayed!
For even the tallest were once small like you,
Just keep growing strong, and soon you'll be blue!"

So with hope and a giggle, the sapling agreed,
"To embrace every storm, I'll plant myself, indeed!"
And who would have known, with joy in their heart,
That the journey's the fun, and that's just the start!

Inked in Nature's Amber Tears

In a forest of laughter, with trees all aglow,
The sap dripped down slow, like a sweet sticky show.
The bees made a buzz, and the ants tapped their feet,
While a frog leaped away, with a wiggle so neat.

"Dance with me, friends!" cried the dapper old bark,
"As we ink funny stories till the sun turns to dark!"
With winks and with chuckles, the forest took flight,
And the twilight was filled with pure whimsical light.

A raccoon with a hat and a voice oh so grand,
Called out all the woodlands to gather and stand.
"Who needs perfect symmetry? Let's celebrate fun!
In this world of odd pleasures, it's all just begun!"

So the forest concluded with frolicsome cheer,
In this haven of humor, they had nothing to fear.
From sap to the shadows, all joy is now clear,
In the ink of their laughter, life blooms every year!

A Tapestry of Flora and Flight

In the garden, bees wear hats,
Pollen pastries – think of that!
Butterflies dance with graceful flair,
While squirrels steal with brazen air.

A turtle once tried running late,
But mistook the gardening gate.
He claimed it was a marathon,
Yet circled back to nap at dawn.

A raccoon chef made quite the mess,
Invented soup, and it was less.
The crickets chirped in pure delight,
Their eyes all twinkling, oh what a sight!

And when the moonlight starts to gleam,
The fireflies throw a silly beam.
They twirl and swirl their light so bright,
It's the waltz of the woodland's night.

Serene Songs of the Sylvan Realm.

The owls wear spectacles to stare,
At rabbits who look quite unaware.
They sing songs of old, with a twist,
While hedgehogs join, shaking their fist!

A fox brought pies to the grand ball,
Yet tripped in his coat and made a call.
The party stopped—what was that sound?
A fox in the ferns, rolling around!

Amidst the trees, where laughter swells,
Chipmunks serve nutty carousels.
They race and chase, a wild, fun scene,
With acorns flying, oh so keen!

When night falls, watch the stars unfold,
As shadows dance in stories told.
Each giggle and grin in the air,
Makes the forest a circus of flair.

Whispers of the Ancient Tree

Beneath the branches, whispers roam,
Where nutballs dream of going home.
A woodpecker joins in on the fun,
Drumming beats beneath the sun.

The wise old tree, with knots and tales,
Tells of squirrels who told tall tales.
A beetle rolls its boulder round,
While saying, 'It's the best in town!'

With laughter ringing through the leaves,
A concert for the autumn eaves.
The breeze hums softly, notes in flight,
As critters dance under starry light.

So join the jamboree tonight,
Where the ancient stand in pure delight.
No worries, just the laughter's clink,
In the glow of moon, we take a wink.

Essence Beneath the Bark

With bark so thick, it's tough to see,
What creatures dwell in jubilee.
A chipmunk made a cozy nook,
And filled it up with every book!

The raccoons took a pizza night,
With toppings that gave quite a fright.
Mushrooms, leaves, and berries mixed,
A feast so odd, the owls were fixed!

As twilight gleamed, all gathered near,
With stories that danced on fluttering ear.
The tree rolled eyes, 'Oh brother' said,
As laughter lit the paths ahead.

So join us here, in giggles vast,
Where shadows whisper, shadows cast.
In nature's arms, the fun won't lack,
For joy is rooted beneath the bark!

The Poetry of Gnarled Roots

In the forest, trees have quirks,
Their roots do all the dirty work.
Whispers echo, leaves conspire,
The trunk's a jester, never tired.

Squirrels giggle, acorns drop,
A woodland dance that just won't stop.
Each twist and turn, a story told,
As branches flex, the tales unfold.

Mushrooms wear their polka dots,
While crickets play their silly slots.
The breeze becomes a cheeky tease,
As nature laughs with utmost ease.

So if you wander down this pass,
Watch for a tree that might just sass.
In gnarled roots and shadows deep,
The poets here have much to peep.

Dreaming of Verdant Verses

Underneath the leafy crowns,
Dreamers spin their fairy gowns.
With words as soft as petals' fall,
Laughter echoes through the hall.

The grass tickles toes and heels,
And chats with wind, with bright appeals.
Flowers nod and roll their eyes,
At forgetful bees and butterflies.

Where sunlight spills like joyful juice,
And every rhyme feels like a truce.
The trees compose their leafy scripts,
As laughter in the air just flips.

So grab a pen, let giggles flow,
In meadows where the wild things grow.
For in this realm of rhyme and fun,
Every line is never done.

Sonnet in the Shadow of the Pines

Beneath the pine's colossal gaze,
A poet plucks the sunlit haze.
With scribbles shared on bark so grand,
A woodsy comedy, quite unplanned.

The needles whisper secret tales,
Of playful winds and froggy scales.
With laughter twinkling in the night,
As owls debate who's wrong or right.

Branching out with curious minds,
Nature's humor, one of a kind.
The squirrels play a card game here,
While shadows cast their quirky cheer.

So here I sit, in this fine nook,
Where every word's a wily hook.
In pines that sway, I seek my muse,
To craft the lines I won't refuse.

Starlit Canopy Chronicles

Under starlight, the tales collide,
Moonbeams dance, chat, and slide.
In this wild, whimsical domain,
Creatures play, not a moment plain.

Bats provide the night's fine swoosh,
While hedgehogs plot a sneaky push.
The crickets strum their nightly tunes,
As raccoons raid the midnight spoons.

Laughter echoes through the trees,
Of soggy socks and playful knees.
Every shadow hides a jest,
In this canopy, life's a fest.

So pull a blanket, stay awhile,
As stars up high outshine the mile.
Join the critters, laugh and bask,
In tales where humor's all you ask.

The Fragrance of Ancient Pines

In a forest of whispers and glee,
Trees chatter about their favorite tea.
They giggle as squirrels race by,
Man, those acorns make quite a pie!

A woodpecker taps in a rhythmic spree,
Who knew that trunks could dance with such glee?
The scent of the branches, oh what a tease,
Makes the rhyme-loving bees feel quite at ease!

Under the shade, critters mime a show,
A frog croaks a verse, and the rabbits follow.
Each breath we take feels light as a breeze,
In this silly world, nothing's a tease!

They toast with acorns, then spill the wine,
Raccoons debate if the moon's just fine.
With laughter and cheers, they banter in jest—
Ah, to be a tree, it's simply the best!

Ballad of the Woodland Nectar

Gather 'round, the trees have a tale,
Of sweet sticky stuff that's known to prevail.
The bees buzz and hum as they plot and they scheme,
Maybe it's time for a sticky-sweet dream!

The owls hoot loudly, "What's this all about?"
"Oh, it's nectar!" the squirrels give a shout.
With acrobatic flips, they gather and sip,
Chasing flavors on a sweet nectar trip!

Then comes a raccoon, with whiskers all sticky,
He grins at the crowd, his antics quite tricky.
"Who needs fine wine when we've got this gold?"
As laughter erupts, the legend is told!

With each little drop, they toast to the night,
The critters all dance in the soft silver light.
A magic so sweet, it rivals the sun—
In this woodland ballet, everyone's won!

Ink from the Heartwood

In the hush of the woods, where secrets abound,
The trees tell their stories, all seasoned and sound.
With bark for my paper and sap for my ink,
I scribble sweet verses, oh what do you think?

A fox fetches quills from a mischievous crow,
While dancing with shadows, they put on a show.
With each drop of liquid, the stories arise,
Of woodland adventures and raccoon spies!

A rat with a beret claims he's quite the bard,
But his rhymes are so wacky, it's truly quite hard.
Yet laughter erupts, it's all in good fun,
A literary jam, oh how it's begun!

With stanzas and couplets, the night stretches wide,
In the heart of the forest, where all dreams abide.
So sip from the stories, let giggles entwine,
In this wooded retreat, everything's divine!

Rhythms in the Bark

Underneath the canopy, a party takes place,
With trees swaying gently, they all keep the pace.
The owls with their hoots, the squirrels with their leaps,
Create a wild rhythm that tickles and creeps!

Beneath the big branches, a raccoon plays drums,
While the hedgehogs tap feet to the beat, oh so fun!
The rhythm gets faster, the critters unite,
As fireflies twinkle and join in the light!

"Oh, look at that squirrel!" the badgers proclaim,
"When he jumps to the beat, he's a wild little flame!"
With laughter and cheers, the bard begins to croon,
This woodland dance party goes on till the moon!

So gather your friends, and let's all make a mark,
In the rhythms of laughter and beats from the bark.
With critters all reveling, we're all quite a sight,
In a forest where fun lasts far into the night!

Whispers in the Conifer Grove

In the grove where pines reside,
The squirrels plot and laugh with pride.
Their acorn hats, a funny sight,
They dance and twirl, oh what delight!

Under branches, shadows play,
A rabbit joins the grand ballet.
With floppy ears that flop around,
He trips and tumbles to the ground.

Fish-lipped trees stretch up so high,
Hoping birds'll land nearby.
But the thieves, those cheeky jays,
Steal their fruit in clever ways!

So when you wander through the green,
Listen close, it's quite the scene.
Nature's jokes and playful tunes,
Make giggles bloom beneath the moons.

Elixir of the Forest Floor

Fungi hats and mossy capes,
Are snails wearing fancy scrapes!
Each patch holds a secret brew,
Where whispers laugh, hearty and true.

A chipmunk sips from puddled rain,
While shuffling 'round, avoiding pain.
He thinks he's fancy, what a clown,
With muddy paws, he hops around!

The bamboo shakes, it starts to sway,
A whisper passes, 'What a day!'
But wind tricks trees with silly must,
As branches sway in gales of gust.

When shadows stretch and twilight nears,
The nightlight bugs lend out their cheers.
Join the fun, just don't ignore,
The laughter bubbling from the floor.

Verses Beneath the Evergreen Canopy

In tangled roots, the critters dwell,
With stories spun, they'd surely tell.
A chipper bird sings off-key,
While bees buzz by, 'It's all for free!'

A porcupine, so prickly proud,
Winks at the clouds, he's feeling loud.
But when a breeze gives him a shove,
He rolls away, not quite in love!

The ferns wave like they're in a cheer,
While beetles march with gusto, dear.
Each step they take, a slapstick show,
In nature's realm, the fun just flows!

So pause awhile beneath this roof,
And let each laugh be your proof.
That nature's lore is wild and free,
With quirky critters, come and see!

A Symphony of Resin and Rhyme

Under boughs with sticky tales,
Where buzzing bees sing of their fails.
A wise old owl hoots, 'What a trap!'
With resin pools, they take a nap!

A hedgehog waddles, what a sight,
With every step, his spines take flight.
He thought he'd found a berry treat,
But slipped instead on sticky feet!

In the rhythm of the gentle breeze,
Cone-funnel hats bring giggles with ease.
The laughter rolls like leaves in fall,
As critters gather for a ball.

So raise a cup to nature's jest,
With every cast, we are all blessed.
In the grove where laughter's prime,
Join the fun in sticky rhyme!

Verses Among the Needles

In the forest choir, they chatter and cheer,
Pine cones beards waving, a sight quite sincere.
A squirrel in tweed with a nutty debate,
Thinks poetry's better than nuts on a plate.

Sap drips like honey, a sticky delight,
Word play in shadows, oh what a sight!
With laughter in branches, they gather and sing,
A symphony spun from a woodpecker's ring.

They argue of stanzas, of rhythm and rhymes,
While bunnies in bonnets keep time to the chimes.
The owls hoot laughter, quite wise, you see,
As verses float down like leaves on a spree.

In this quirky glen where the funny things grow,
The poets are critters with quite the fine show.
Join in the frolic, don't leave out your quill,
For joy's in the ink, and the trees have the thrill!

When Flora Becomes Verse

When daisies discuss the latest in style,
Their petals a-rustle, they giggle a while.
The roses roll eyes, with a prickly retort,
Claiming violets are just a flowerly sport.

A daffodil dips, like a dancer in flight,
While ferns tell tall tales of the moon's silvery light.
They rhyme 'neath the sun in a quirky parade,
As bees buzz along, orchestrating street trade.

Petunias in tutus, with flair on display,
Bop to the music, oh what a bouquet!
With lilacs in cliques sharing secrets galore,
The garden's a stage; who could ask for more?

Whispers of blossoms, so sprightly and clear,
In this florid theater, laughter's sincere.
Join their capers, feel free to immerse,
In the charm of the blooms, where nature's the verse.

The Language of the Leaf

Leaves gossip in circles, with whispers and laughs,
Telling tales of the wind and the scatter of halves.
With rustling banter, they sway side to side,
While acorns in hats play the wise little guide.

A maple in red tells a story so grand,
While the birch on the side just can't understand.
"Why not just sway, and enjoy what you got?"
Says the little green shoot, in a voice cold and hot.

Each twig feels the rhythm, each leaf knows the beat,
As they dance in the sunlight, none missing a feat.
They turn up their edges, and giggle with glee,
For the humor of nature is spot on, you see.

In this canopy theater, no giants, just fun,
A show where the plants outshine everyone.
So listen, take note, of their leafy dares,
For within their laughter, true magic ensnares.

Elysian Murmurs of the Wild

In the heart of the wild, where critters convene,
Laughter echoes loud in a somewhat bizarre scene.
A hare tells a legend of how he outpaced,
A tortoise with style, with not an ounce of haste.

The branches all lean in to catch the next line,
While raccoons in tuxes sip berries like wine.
The jays drop their gossip from heights up above,
Creating a ruckus of nature's own love.

A fox dressed in velvet gives tips for a dance,
While a badger in spectacles takes quite the chance.
They twirl and they prance, in a woodland ballet,
As shadows grow long, bidding daylight away.

In this reveling realm, where the wild cheers and stands,
Each moment's a jest, crafted by nature's own hands.
So come join the revel with wildness and glee,
For laughter in Nature is the way it should be!

Notes from a Timbered Soul

In the forest where I twirl,
Trees gossip and leaves unfurl.
Squirrels debating on the best pine,
Their acorn stash, oh so divine.

Mossy logs are my comfy seat,
Critters serenade me, oh what a treat!
A chipmunk challenges my rhyming scheme,
I chuckle and ponder, is this a dream?

The wind whispers jokes, oh so sly,
Telling tales of branches that reach for the sky.
Nature's comedy, a delightful jest,
Among the trees, I feel so blessed.

So here I dwell, with humor galore,
Among the trees, I laugh and explore.
A timbered soul, with a grin so wide,
In this woodsy world, I take great pride.

The Poetry of Shaded Whispers

In a glade where shadows play,
Trees conspire in a comical way.
Leaves giggle as they dance in the breeze,
Barking up jokes that tickle with ease.

Pine needles drop like unexpected laughs,
Falling softly, nature's silly half.
A woodpecker drums out a witty beat,
Nature's own band, oh what a treat!

Boughs sway to verses no one knows,
Each rhyme a twist in the stories that grows.
In this woodsy nook of lighthearted cheer,
The orchestra of nature is perfectly clear.

So I'll pen my thoughts under boughs so stout,
Where laughter bounces and worries pout.
In whispered tones, the trees can declare,
That humor blooms bright, beyond compare.

Resinous Reveries at Dusk

As the sun dips low with a wink in its eye,
The trees trade stories as time drifts by.
A hermit crab sought my opinion today,
On how best to express what crabs want to say.

The smell of pine mixed with laughter sprung,
My thoughts get tangled, but I'm still young.
A crow caws jokes that make no sense,
In this quirky audience, I find recompense.

Sap oozes slowly, oh what a scene,
Like life's little mishaps wrapped up in green.
Each drip a giggle from the high timber,
And as night falls, my heart grows limber.

So here I sit, in this resinous glow,
Breaking out rhymes from the moments below.
In the twilight hum, I find delight,
In the forest's folly, under starlight.

Verses of the Canopy's Embrace

Under a canopy, laughter is stored,
Where branches plot and their humor's adored.
A raccoon recites a ridiculous rhyme,
While a rabbit audition for the next primetime.

To each whisper, I lend my ear,
As trees giggle, shedding their fear.
Buds burst open to join in the jest,
In this lush comedy, I feel so blessed.

The woodwind tunes elicit a snicker,
As I try to catch each playful flicker.
Feathers and fur, a fanciful crowd,
Helping the forest's laughter grow loud.

So let me linger in this woodland spree,
Where the verses bloom high and wild and free.
In this embrace, the world feels right,
Among these giggles, well into the night.

Syllables from the Wildwood

In the woods, a squirrel prances,
Chasing shadows, taking chances.
Whispers flutter, giggles tease,
All the trees share secret keys.

Mushrooms dance in silly shoes,
While the rabbits sing the blues.
Fireflies fashion glow-in-the-dark,
Bouncing round like a bright spark.

The owls hoot a wacky tune,
As raccoons join beneath the moon.
Branches sway, they laugh and sway,
Nature's jesters at their play.

Leaves confetti, fall like rain,
Who knew woods could be so vain?
Sing with joy, let voices clash,
In the wildwood, make a splash!

The Forest's Lullaby

Amidst the trees, a fox lays low,
Singing softly, 'Let's take it slow.'
Frogs croak back in harmony,
With crickets playing symphony.

A bear forgot where it left its hat,
While raccoons plot their next big spat.
Suddenly, a twig snaps tight,
All the critters take to flight!

Deer prance lightly, dodge a snail,
As squirrels gather without fail.
Nature's humor, can't be beat,
With every twist, a funny feat.

Breezes chuckle through the leaves,
Planting giggles in the eaves.
Sleepy woods, a cheeky place,
Where every critter wears a face!

Sapling Dreams in Twilight

Under stars, a dream unfolds,
Saplings whisper tales retold.
A chipmunk's hat is on too tight,
He spins around, oh what a sight!

A hedgehog rolls, loses track,
Mistaking shadows as a snack.
With a twirl, he bumps a tree,
Giggling hard, as all agree.

Twilight's cloak drapes soft and warm,
Trees dance lightly, breaking norm.
Laughing branches sway and tease,
In the cool with every breeze.

Fireflies flicker, mischief bright,
Lighting up the forest night.
In a world spun tight with glee,
Every creature's fancy-free!

Ode to the Bough and Breeze

Ode to the bough that bends with grace,
And the breeze that quickens the pace.
Squirrels hide their nuts away,
With faces bright, they laugh and play.

An owl wears glasses too large,
Claiming wisdom, tries to charge.
While chipmunks gossip, side by side,
Holding secrets they can't abide.

A branch breaks loose, a wrestling match,
Woodpecker cheers, a cheeky catch.
Nature's folly, oh so sweet,
Who knew woodlands could compete?

So here's to whispers in the wild,
Every moment, nature's child.
Boughs and breezes laugh and sing,
In the forest, joy's the thing!

Branches That Write

In the forest of puns, where trees start to jest,
The branches get scribbles, they think they're the best.
They cover their bark with tales from the past,
And giggles erupt when the light breezes blast.

The squirrels take notes on acorn-based lore,
While rabbits hold court by the old wooden door.
With every small quip, the trunks start to shake,
As nature reveals what good humor can make.

The whispering leaves join a banter so light,
Turning shadows to jokes that tickle the night.
Even moss joins in with a quippy retort,
Each knot in the wood is a wayward report.

So next when you wander through green-riddled rays,
Listen to trees weave their whimsical ways.
For humor abounds in the stories they share,
In branches that write, life's laughter is rare.

A Lament for the Lost Roots

Oh, roots that once tangled in the earth's merry fray,
Now stuck in their shoes, what a curious play!
They long for soft soil, but strut in their boots,
Complaining of grass stains, lamenting their snoots.

"Remember," they sigh, "all the fun that we had,
Dancing in dirt like a party gone rad?"
With every small quiver, they miss their old home,
Instead, they throw tantrums, refusing to roam.

That fibrous old squad, they yearn for the dew,
But prance in their heels, doing tango or two.
"They never will know how we swayed with the breeze,
Now look at us tripping on fancy tall trees!"

So if you find roots in a bind, take heed,
Give warmth to their troubles, plant smiles with speed.
For deep in the ground, there's a joyful pursuit,
As roots can still chuckle in soil, not just soot.

The Green Ink of Earth's Rhapsody

With ink made of chlorophyll, scribes in the shade,
Trees twirl their quills, crafting tales unafraid.
Each leaf's witty quip is a fragrant delight,
As branches compose under soft moonlit night.

"Page one," they decree, "let's start with a joke,
Of the squirrel who thought he could outpace a croak."
The narratives flutter like butterflies bright,
As the ink spills with laughter, a wild, joyful sight.

Beneath all the laughter, a wisdom runs deep,
As roots settle tales that the winds softly weep.
There's magic at play with each quirk they entwine,
The forest's own bard, with a punchline divine.

So gather, dear friends, for a verse-full of cheer,
Join in with the trees, let your worries disappear.
In the green ink of life, everyone's welcome,
For joy's just a pattern in nature's grand spectrum.

Whispers of Wood and Wonder

In the thicket of giggles, the trees hold their breath,
For whispers of mischief herald life from the swath.
"Did you hear," they confide, "about the old pine?
He tried to be trendy, adorned in moonshine!"

The firs roll their rings, sharing tales from the past,
Where laughter was golden, and friendships held fast.
A quip from their bark makes the willows all sway,
While oaks join the chorus, "What else can we say?"

Caught in this jest, every bough starts to sway,
They dream of the moments that brightened their day.
From saplings to elders, the humor flows free,
In whispers of wood, where all laugh soulfully.

So wander through forests, where joy grants a spark,
Embrace all the quirks by the trunks in the dark.
For humor's a treasure that nature endows,
In whispers of wonder, let laughter arouse.

The Narrative of Nature's Tapestry

In the woods where the giggles roam,
A squirrel found a nut, thought it a dome.
He danced with joy, round the tallest tree,
Believing he'd found his new abode, you see.

The leaves whispered secrets, oh so sly,
As the owls rolled their eyes, let out a sigh.
"Nuts acting grand, we've seen it before,
Why can't they just eat? What is this encore?"

The ladybug laughed, perched on a leaf,
She claimed to be queen, oh what a belief!
But when a breeze came, down she did plummet,
"Let's revise this role, and spare me the summit!"

A moth threw a party, inviting the night,
But forgot to ask the moon for some light.
They danced in the dark, oh what a display,
With shadows as partners, they twirled away.

Sap and Stories of Time

A tree once thought it was quite the sage,
Sharing its wisdom as birds would engage.
"Life's a long journey," it rumbled in glee,
As the branches nodded, just as wise as he!

The beetles and bugs, they gathered around,
Each one with tales that they had simply found.
A worm spoke of dirt, as thrilling as clay,
"Such drama it brings!" he cheered, "Hooray!"

But when a pinecone fell, with a thud,
It claimed to give wisdom, hang on to this bud!
"Lessons of falling," it said with a breeze,
"Just land on your feet, stay grounded with ease!"

The laughter erupted, it rang through the trees,
The stories continued, carried by leaves.
In a forest filled with quirks and delight,
Who knew that the bark could be such a fright?

Twilight's Gentle Sonnet

As twilight arrived, the stars felt so shy,
They hid behind clouds, peeking up high.
"Shall we play hide and seek?" one cheeky comet said,
While the moon just rolled eyes and shook his big head.

The crickets formed bands, with grass blades as strings,
Creating a symphony of silly things.
"Let's play the tune of a thousand dates!"
Cried a firefly loud, illuminating fates.

The shadows joined in, doing the tango,
As wisps of the night twirled with a dango.
While owls in the wisdom sung duets by voice,
The forest was nuts, but oh, what a choice!

When bedtime hit, and the laughter grew dim,
The moon grinned and said, "Let's give it a rim!"
For in every star, there's a tale to unfold,
In the twilight's embrace, every dream is retold.

The Enigma of the Forest's Call

A fox took a stroll, in search of a clue,
He sought out mystery in morning dew.
"Does the grass giggle or whisper it's wise?"
He pondered aloud, with bright, curious eyes.

An acorn chuckled, "You're barking up dreams,
I'm the king of the forest, or so it seems!"
All the rabbits snickered, the deer took a bow,
"Does anyone here take a lesson from now?"

The trees leaned in closer, with leaves all a-flutter,
As a wise old crow let out a loud mutter.
"Life's but a riddle, with each twist and turn,
Find joy in the quirks, and laughter will burn!"

The sun set its glow on that quirky crew,
With secrets and giggles found deep in the blue.
And the forest, a canvas where stories unfold,
Made even the starlight feel goofy and bold.

Echoes of Nature's Ink

In the forest where jokes reside,
Trees giggle as squirrels collide.
Pine needles whisper, 'Don't be a bore,'
While branches creak, 'We need more!'

Bunny hops with a witty flair,
He tells the trees, 'You wouldn't dare!'
Leaves chuckle softly, 'Oh, what a sight!'
As nature's pranks dance in the light.

Bark's Secret Language

The bark has tales that tickle the ear,
In layered grooves, laughter is near.
Whispers of mischief, old tales they tell,
Of acorns that fell, then rang like a bell.

A woodpecker's tap is a rhythm divine,
Knocking on secrets like, 'Hey, life's fine!'
The sap flows slowly, what's in store?
Perhaps a sweet joke, or maybe more!

Veins of Evergreen Poetry

In every vein, a punchline beats,
Evergreen laughs, oh, what a treat!
Moss agrees, with a sly little grin,
'Life's a jest, let the fun begin!'

Ferns flutter their fronds with delight,
As sunbeams chuckle, chasing the night.
Nature's prose, cheeky and bright,
Leaves fluttering, oh what a sight!

Timeless Tides of Woodland

Woodland waves rock a rhythm so quirky,
As trees sway gently, feeling quite perky.
With roots intertwined, they share a laugh,
'Why'd the tree cross the road?'—no photograph!

A deer rolls eyes at this timeless jest,
While shadows dance, so snug in their rest.
Nature's comedy, never too trite,
In the embrace of the night, all feels right.

Bark Poems Beneath the Stars

In the night sky, squirrels dance,
Chasing moonbeams, taking a chance.
Their acorns like diamonds, all in a row,
Who knew they were such high-class folk, though?

The trees whisper tales with a crooked grin,
As the owls hoot softly, where to begin?
Beneath leafy boughs, the laughter grows wide,
While critters recite rhymes with great pride.

Branches all wiggle, as if saying 'Hi!'
Nature's own jesters, oh my oh my!
With roots underground joining in the jest,
The bark makes it clear, we are truly blessed.

So lift up your heads, let the starlight peak,
Where laughter and trees find the fun that we seek.
With a chuckle on leaves and a giggle on air,
Each shadow beneath holds a story to share.

Nature's Breath in Every Stanza

Whispers of winds weave tales ever sly,
Leaves tickle the bark, 'Oh my, oh my!'
Branches chuckle low, as they swayed and bent,
Tickling roots who simply can't pay rent.

A deer in the moonlight, sporting a bow tie,
Winks at the hedgehog, as they stroll by.
The brook giggles wildly, splashes with glee,
Making jest of the rocks, 'Try catching me!'

Flowers form a chorus, with petals all bright,
Playing hide and seek till the fall of the night.
Each beetle, each breeze, full of quirky delight,
Every twinkle and rustle, a wonderful sight.

In this rhythmic realm where the wild things play,
Nature's breath sings lullabies all through the day.
A merry cacophony of joy we find,
With every turn of phrase, laughter intertwined.

Fables of the Branching Path

Down the winding trail, critters convene,
Sharing their secrets, all well unseen.
With a hop and a skip, the bunny narrates,
The fox deals in puns, nothing resonates.

Tales of the twisted vines circle around,
Where mushrooms wear caps like kings in the mound.
The pebbles all chuckle at stories they hear,
From squirrels who boast of their wintertime cheer.

The trees hold their sides, shaking their leaves,
As a skunk tells a story of sinus thieves.
With every bark, there's a punchline to catch,
These whimsical tales are a perfect mismatch.

So wander along this path lined with glee,
Join in the fun, you'll feel so carefree.
Nature's own fables, a comedy of sorts,
Where every twig whispers of life and retorts.

Metaphors in the Meadow's Embrace

In the meadow's warmth, the daisies collide,
Dancing and twirling, with no place to hide.
A butterfly laughs, its wings all aglow,
While ants in a line are preparing a show.

With dandelion wishes, the fairies conspire,
To make each wish come true, they never tire.
Bees buzz with humor, a sweet little sting,
As the grass beneath folds, it begins to sing.

From petals to pollen, each role is precise,
A comedy troupe, nature's own paradise.
Every quirk and giggle beneath the sky bright,
In the soft summer breeze, everything feels right.

So gather your thoughts in this whimsical place,
Revel in laughter, and joyfully chase.
With metaphors blooming, life's funny display,
In the meadow's embrace, let's dance and sway.

The Charm of Evergreen Melodies

In a forest bright, a tune takes flight,
A squirrel sings with all its might,
The trees sway gently, dance and clap,
While birds roll dice in a game of crap.

A chipmunk jigs, on logs it struts,
The pine needles fall, a stage for nuts,
With every twist, a laugh it brings,
Nature's concert of silly things.

The wind hums low, a cheeky breeze,
As leaves share gossip, dance with ease,
Fungi giggle as they sprout,
What a show, without a doubt!

Each note is light, a merry tease,
The critters break all boundaries,
In this wild realm, with laughs to share,
Evergreen beats beyond compare.

Ink-stained Memories of Moss

In the quiet glades, a raccoon scribes,
With inky paws and no clear vibes,
It pens a tale of nighttime blunders,
Of shiny trash and hidden wonders.

The mushrooms boast of how they sprout,
While crickets chirp, in and out,
A tapestry, beneath the shade,
Of silly stories, nature made.

Moss explored, with scribbled lines,
Of squabbles, fumbles, and sticky pines,
The forest laughs, till stars align,
An ode to oddities, quite divine.

With every squish upon the ground,
The echoes of fun are all around,
These wild tales, so absurd and sweet,
Ink-stained memories beneath our feet.

A Soliloquy of Twisted Branches

A branch speaks softly, a tale unrolled,
Of a wise old tree, quite proud and bold,
With knots and turns, it spins a yarn,
Of wobbling winds that leave a scar.

"Listen close, for I have seen,"
"Frogs in top hats and bears in green!"
The laughter of trunks, echoing wide,
As bark-clad creatures run and hide.

Twisted limbs, they weave a plot,
Of woodland antics, a quirky lot,
With squirrels swapping leaves for tricks,
And owls wearing sunglasses, just for kicks.

So gather 'round, let's share the glee,
Of branches crooning their wild decree,
In this realm of whimsy, laughter's art,
A soliloquy that warms the heart.

Chants Beneath the Tender Leaves

Beneath soft canopies, whispers grow,
With giggles ripe, they start the show,
A chorus of critters, all aglow,
In a symphony only they know.

Grasshoppers leap with twirls so fine,
While beetles chime in, oh so divine,
The melody of mischief, loud and clear,
As peeking cats cause a raucous cheer.

Leaves clap in rhythm, a gentle sound,
Nature's choir, all around,
With each flutter, a chuckle born,
In this realm, where fun is worn.

So join the dance, let joy take flight,
With every chant, we feel the light,
Beneath the leaves, let laughter weave,
In harmony, we all believe.

www.ingramcontent.com/pod-product-compliance
Lightning Source LLC
Chambersburg PA
CBHW072138200426
43209CB00050B/119